'My best wishes for the book.'
   – Ratan N Tata, Chairman Emeritus, Tata Sons

'...crafted a lovely story around luxury in India from the Maharajas to the newer rich... a great read for anyone interested in the science of vanity and what makes luxury tick. All luxury brand wants to be aspirational without alienating people or being aloof. This book has many illustrative examples to satiate your curiosity.'
   – D Shivakumar, Chairman and CEO, PepsiCo India

'...a delightfully-written book on luxury brands and luxury consumers... rich in anecdotes... A wonderful read.'
   – Bibek Debroy, Author, Economist, Academic and Member of NITI Aayog

'...Mahul has been able to bring in new thoughts, ideas and perspectives. I like the innovative measures he has created... This will be a great measure for luxury brands to understand the desirability of their brand.'
   – Nirvik Singh, Chairman and CEO, Grey Advertising APAC

'...a gifted writer passionate about luxury... gives a very unique perspective to luxury... a great read...'
– Harshavardhan Neotia, Past President FICCI and Chairman, Ambuja Neotia Group

'...a prolific writer... has been able to introduce some unconventional ideas and thoughts... Decoding Luxe will be greatly appreciated.'
– Hemant Kanoria, CMD, SREI Infrastructure Finance Ltd

'I love the way Mahul deconstructs the mystical world of luxury with his simple, direct, matter-of-fact lucid style of narration... a very well written book...'
– Arnab Chakraborty, National Director, UN-Empretec Programme for India, UNCTAD

'...Mahul's style has been very refreshing and easily digestible. He has managed to give a personality to luxury in the book... a fantastic read.'
– Namit Bajoria, Director, Kutchina

'...one-of-its-kind holistic book on this subject of luxury... a great handbook for luxury brands... captures many unconventional and rather counter-intuitive perspectives...'
– Ambarish Dasgupta, Former President, Bengal Chamber of Commerce and Industries

'...I applaud Mahul for his brilliant attempt at decoding luxury and presenting a holistic view on this subject with a focus on India... a must read.'
– Sidharth Pansari, Director, Primarc

Decoding Luxe

MAHUL BRAHMA

Srishti
PUBLISHERS & DISTRIBUTORS

Srishti Publishers & Distributors
Registered Office: N-16, C.R. Park
New Delhi – 110 019
Corporate Office: 212A, Peacock Lane
Shahpur Jat, New Delhi – 110 049
editorial@srishtipublishers.com

First published by
Srishti Publishers & Distributors in 2017

10 9 8 7 6 5 4 3 2 1

This is a work of non-fiction, based on the author's research in the field of luxury products and studies associated with it.

The author asserts the moral right to be identified as the author of this work.

Printed and bound in India

Contents

CONTENTS

List of Illustrations

Image 1: *Cartier's necklace for Maharaja of Patiala's crown, which weighs 962.25 carats with 2,930 De-Beers diamonds.*

Image 2: *In 1928, the Maharaja of Jammu & Kashmir placed orders for custom-made thirty trunks from luggage maker Louis Vuitton over a period of six months.*

Image 3: *A Cartier Pathere ring, a timeless icon for the company, representing what's both predatory and elegant.*

Image 4: *"Money can't buy happiness. But, somehow, it is more comfortable to cry in a Lamborghini than on a bicycle."*

Foreword

Luxury is no more an alien word for an average Indian. The ever-swelling middle class too is smitten by the romance of the super brands – be it a Louis Vuitton or a Burberry. Gone are the days when Indians travelled abroad to bring back an iconic sling bag or a trench coat. With the number of millionaires rocketing over the past five years, these brands are now opening shop within the country. Mahul's book is a seminal and in-depth work that feels the pulse, not just of the luxury industry, but also of the consumer. He does a huge favour to both – makes life easier for the brands by telling them how to tap further into the Indian psyche on the one hand, and whetting the appetite of buyers excited by luxury on the other. Mahul's style is lucid, his analysis impeccable. This book is a must have.

Kounteya Sinha
The Times of India, United Kingdom

Foreword

In 2002, my newsroom colleague and I won a major quizzing event. Since the contest was organized to raise funds for charity, we did not receive any cash prize. Instead, we were handed vouchers to buy books and a few clothes. One such voucher was from a luxury clothing brand that made some exquisite formal suits. The value of the voucher could not have been even half of the lowest-priced jacket in the store at a luxury hotel in South Mumbai. Yet, my wife insisted that we both go to the store, to at least see what is on offer.

As we entered the place, I was nervous. This was the first time I'd entered a luxury brand store. My anxiety, I would find out, was not without reason. The store staff, adept at decoding body language and the income group of the walk-in customer, talked to me with utter disdain. It made me even more anxious. I had cold sweat over my forehead. In the end, from what seemed like an hour-long ordeal, all I could take from there was a worn-out green tweed jacket. I could sense the smirks of the sales staff while they were packing it, and I got the feeling they must have had a hearty laugh when I left, and then, for good measure, gone home and related the story to their families to entertain them at dinner. Thirteen years later, I am still traumatized by that incident. I have not re-entered a luxury store since then, even though I know I can now afford a few of the products on display.

I know I am not alone.

Why do luxury brands evoke such a response from India's rising middle class? Is it the prices? Is there some invisible force shield outside each store that prevents us from entering it? Or is it because, more often than not, the sales staff is better dressed than us? I have no answer to these questions. Yet, I also know that luxury brands in India have only gone from strength to strength in the last decade. According to a report in Mumbai edition of *The Hindu* (30 December 2015), at least five global luxury brands – Ferrari, Christian Dior, La Perla, Jimmy Choo, and Bulgari – have re-entered India to take advantage of rising incomes and a robust GDP growth rate. Surely there's a market. It's an enigmatic market, yes, as no one seems to have calculated the exact value of luxe brand sales in India, but the products are out there, staring at our faces.

Therefore, my friend Mahul's attempt to understand the dynamics of this market seems timely. There is no one definition of luxury, but you know what luxury is when you see it. It is this vague, yet seemingly rational definition of the term that we could possibly go with. But this book is not just about the market for luxury. When I read it, I was pleasantly surprised to find that Mahul has worked hard to decode even the customer. In a market that is ready to explode, understanding the customer could well be the key to retaining them, and for expanding the scope of the luxury segment itself. Otherwise, as in the case with me after the clothing store experience in 2002, the luxury market could lose several potential buyers. Forever.

Sachin Kalbag
Editor-*The Hindu*, Mumbai

Preface

The Quest for Luxe

My quest for luxury began two decades ago, with an inheritance from my grandfather: his Omega Seamaster manual-wind mechanical wristwatch. I always held it very close to my heart, not because it was an Omega limited edition, but because it was my grandfather's last gift. I was fascinated with its movements and complications. Even today, I never forget to wind it, every day. But it is since then that I started exploring the world of fine craftsmanship and luxury.

Over the years, my quest has helped me explore the various facets of the dazzle-luxe. The rich history of craftsmanship, the heritage, the sheer finesse with which an exquisite handcrafted piece is created – every bit of it is a treasure trove for a storyteller.

Unfortunately, the literature on luxury is very limited, globally, and writers have mostly focused on cataloguing luxury products and showcasing them. There was an urgent need to narrate a wonderful tale of luxe – capturing this wonderful dazzle in a holistic way, unveiling its various facets.

My columns for *The Economic Times – ET Retail* have been a great avenue for narrating the untold luxury story. Whether you can afford it or not, you can always appreciate it.

However, through my columns I was not able to paint a holistic, all-encompassing picture of luxe. I felt the need to pen a book that captures the essence of luxury and its long-standing romance with India.

This book is a result of that quest on which I had embarked on two decades ago. It has been a great adventure and I want more and more people to set sail.

Dear reader, I welcome you to join me in this quest for luxury.

A note from the author

Dear reader, if you're wondering what this book is going to be about, let me give you a small glimpse of it from my perspective, and tell you how it came to be. This book essentially explores various facets of luxury brands, which used to be a niche market, but only till some time back. As the realms of luxury and affordability fuse with common people, this book takes a strategic, behavioural, historical, experiential, demographical, psychological, dynamic, mechanical, and also a philosophical look at what constitutes luxe or dazzle.

It is a bible for all stakeholders of luxury brands – owner, custodian, retailer, connoisseur as well as student – helping them understand and formulate, with a historical perspective, an effective strategy for conceiving, positioning, placing, promoting and pricing these luxury products.

With the ebbing Chinese luxury story, most luxury goods providers – including world's biggest luxury group LVMH (Moët Hennessy Louis Vuitton SE) – are shifting focus to the growing luxury consumer base in India, which is poised to grow at 25% from 2013 till 2018, and is likely to touch $18-billion mark from the ongoing level of $14 billion.

The book narrates the story of the Great Indian Middle Class, their aspirations, and how, contrary to popular perception, they are the biggest drivers of luxury brands in India.

Decoding Luxe traces the journey towards democratisation of luxury from royal exclusivity. Today, with the New Maharajas, even royalty is just a swipe away.

And then there's the dark side of luxe and the great escape.

Luxury consumers, although classified into Experientialists, Connoisseurs, Flaunters and Aesthetes, show mixed and overlapping characteristics. The only thing that is all-pervasive is perhaps "price-sensitivity".

You will also get to know of an entire industry working on luxury counterfeits available online and how e-commerce has failed to repeat its success story with luxury brands.

I have also tried to give herein the life cycle of a luxury brand, its Seven Ages, as well as its Ego. You will come to know how over a period of time a brand or product comes to acquire a life of its own, influencing and affecting the producers, sellers and consumers alike.

However, this book is not at all about product reviews, which is what is largely considered as luxury writing in India and abroad. This book will not tell you what to buy and from where to buy it. No! This isn't a catalogue of luxury goods and boutiques.

Decoding Luxe takes you on a quest through dreams, aspirations, contradictions, myths, royalty, and realities that shroud this very mysterious element called luxury.

Acknowledgements

I thank you, dear reader, from the bottom of my heart for choosing *Decoding Luxe*. This book wouldn't have been possible without your love and support.

I am thankful to Mr Ratan N Tata (Chairman Emeritus, Tata Sons) for being such an inspiration and for making time to convey his best wishes for the book.

I thank two of my former colleagues and great friends, Mr Sachin Kalbag (*The Hindu*) and Mr Kounteya Sinha (*The Times of India*) for writing the two forewords. I couldn't have imagined a better introduction for my book.

My heartfelt thanks to the esteemed authors Mr Kunal Basu, Mr Bibek Debroy, and Mr Sarnath Banerjee for writing such lovely praises for the book. You have always inspired me.

ACKNOWLEDGEMENTS

Mr D Shivakumar (Chairman, PepsiCo India), thanks so much for your encouragement and support. I pray all my readers love the book the way you do. Humbled.

I am grateful to my former bosses Mr Sanjiv Goenka (Chairman, RP-SG Group) and Mr Harshavardhan Neotia (Chairman, Ambuja Neotia Group) for always being there for me as my pillars of strength.

Mr Nirvik Singh (Chairman, Grey Advertising APAC), you and your feedback have always given me a great perspective and have been a great source of inspiration.

I am grateful to Mr Hemant Kanoria (CMD, SREI Infrastructure), Mr Namit Bajoria (Director, Kutchina), Mr Arnab Chakraborty (UNCTAD), Mr Ambarish Dasgupta (Past President, BCC&I), and Mr Sidharth Pansari (Director, Primarc) for the encouraging words. They mean a lot to me and to my readers.

I am thankful to Mr Vinaya Varma (CEO of mjunction), Mr Viresh Oberoi (Former CEO and MD of mjunction), and Mr Sandipan Chakravortty (Chairman of mjunction) for their encouragement and support.

Thanks to Mr TV Narendran (MD of Tata Steel) and Mr Sanjay Kapoor (MD of Genesis Luxury) for your encouragement for the book and for being a critic of my luxury columns. Thanks Dr Mukund Rajan (Former Brand Custodian of Tata Sons) and Mr Harish Bhat (Brand Custodian of Tata Sons and Chairman of Tata Global Beverages) for your best wishes.

Special thanks to the organization which made me a journalist, a luxury columnist and now an author, *The Economic Times*. Thanks *ET Retail* for giving me the

ACKNOWLEDGEMENTS

opportunity to share my thoughts and ideas in my column on luxury brands. It has given me the courage to put together new insights in the form of a book on luxury and share it with a wider audience.

Thanks to my friend Indranil Bhoumik for the wonderful photograph.

I extend my gratitude to all my friends and well-wishers for their support and blessings.

My heartfelt thanks to Srishti Publishers and Arup Bose for making this dream come true.

Thank you Jojo (Mr Jaideep Bose, Editorial Director, *The Times of India*) for making me a journalist, and Jehangir Pocha (former Editor, *Business World*) for introducing me to the world of luxury.

Thanks baba for your blessings; you were gone too soon.

A special thanks to my significant better half Sabiya. This book wouldn't have been possible without you. Your book cover design and the illustrations have given a new dimension to the book.

And last but not the least, I am grateful to God Almighty for being so kind and generous, always. I feel loved and blessed.

To send in your observations and feedback, write to me at mahul@mahulbrahma.com.

Mahul Brahma

Decoding Luxe

"Give 'em the old razzle dazzle
Razzle Dazzle 'em
Give 'em an act with lots of flash in it
And the reaction will be passionate ..."

– 'Razzle Dazzle' song from *Chicago (1998)*

Image 1: *Cartier's necklace for Maharaja of Patiala's crown, which weighs 962.25 carats with 2,930 De-Beers diamonds.*

What is luxury? No matter how obvious the question might seem, it demands some contemplation. What does luxury mean to you? Expensive? Exorbitant? Unaffordable? The word luxury has its origin in "luxe", which means "dazzle". So technically, anything that dazzles you is luxury and it is this dazzle that commands the premium. Whether you call that dazzle "brand equity" or "razzle dazzle" is completely your call.

Let's take a sneak peek into the age-old love affair between branded luxury and our great nation of royalty. In the 1920s, 20% of Rolls Royce's global sales were from India. In 1926, the Maharaja of Patiala commissioned Cartier, its largest till date, to remodel his crown jewels, which included the 234.69 carat De Beers diamond (see Image 1). The result was a breathtaking Patiala necklace weighing 962.25 carats with 2,930 diamonds. In 1928, the Maharaja of Jammu & Kashmir placed orders for custom-made thirty trunks from luggage maker Louis Vuitton (LV) over a period of six months (see page 6). Not to mention that a certain Nizam had procured fifty Harley Davidsons for his postmen to deliver his messages (see page 93).

However, the scenario took a complete turn post-Independence and anything remotely opulent was frowned upon, as India flirted with socialism. It was only in the few recent decades, that there was a shift, and the New Maharajas – industrialists, entrepreneurs, professionals, and the rural rich – started blatantly adoring and flaunting all things luxurious. In fact, just like China, the growth in luxury sector is fuelled by the new, young, upper middle class with a tendency to spend rather than save. They are the new generation, first-time customers for luxury products. But India also has other growth drivers, which are not at all conventional and are quite counter-intuitive – The Great Indian Middle Class or GIMC.

However, with the China luxury growth tide ebbing, India has become the focus of major luxury retailers and brands. In India, both conventional and unconventional forces have been acting as drivers. So here it is both old money as well as new money, coupled with the GIMC aspirations, that drive the growth story.

Relativity

"When a man sits with a pretty girl for an hour, it seems like a minute. But let him sit on a hot stove for a minute and it's longer than any hour. That's relativity."

– Albert Einstein

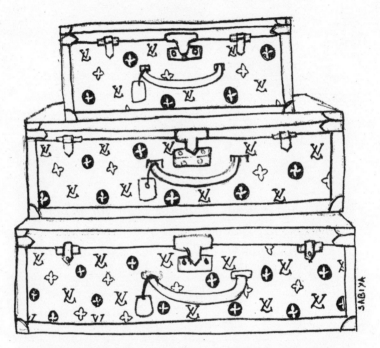

Image 2: *In 1928, the Maharaja of Jammu & Kashmir placed orders for custom-made thirty trunks from luggage maker Louis Vuitton over a period of six months.*

Luxury is relative. The luxe quotient (or LQ as it is referred to) and luxe factor – both measures that I have created to measure this dazzle and will be discussed in detail in the chapter "Measuring Luxe" (see page 85)– are fundamentally relative. However, what dazzles you may not dazzle me. Also the degree of dazzle becomes a key differentiator.

Let me elaborate the degrees to which the razzle-dazzle differs with a few Indian examples. I drool over a Cartier Panthere ring (see page 10), or a LV hot-stamped trunk. For me, that is luxury. However, making an apple to apple comparison, my dazzle just seems lacking any lustre when we look at the way the Richie Riches of our great nation of the poor have dabbled in luxury – be it the Maharaja of Patiala Bhupinder Singh's Cartier crown with 234.69 carat De Beers diamond, or the Maharaja of Jammu & Kashmir Hari Singh's thirty customized LV trunks (see Image 2), one of which is still on display at one of the LV stores.

Talking of LV trunks, let me share some more interesting facets of this long and loving courtship of LV with Indian royalty. Louis Vuitton was unique in its use of valuable materials and precious leather. The luxury house was always able to serve special requests from the Indian Maharajas, no matter how extraordinary, elaborate, or detailed the demands were. A certain Maharaja had ordered all the trunks imaginable for the most diverse of items – golf clubs, turbans, decorations, polo sticks, horseshoes, colonial helmets, among others.

And then there were LV trunks meant for first-aid, files, cleaning shoes, typewriters, as well as Deauville and Beauvais suitcases adapted to lunch cases, and canvas casing for even a crib. All had a distinctive stamp – "J & K", with a diagonal stripe, the hotstamp.

Sayajirao Gaekwad III of Baroda, a connoisseur of luxury brands, with a special liking for LV, even had Morocco leather cases covered in Lozine ranging from his toiletry accessories to keeping tea.

The degree of dazzle is a crucial enabler that every luxury brand needs to understand very clearly.

There is no "one size fits all" when it comes to luxury branding. It's a bespoke world, where customization – to make every customer feel special – is everything, to justify the brand premium in pricing.

So mixing the right portion of the snob-value is by far the biggest challenge for a luxury brand. It's not about alienating others, but it needs to position itself exclusively. The right portion is the magic potion; more of a co-existence of the presence and the absence of snob-quotient, side by side.

Some of you enjoy this magic potion. With low-hanging accessories like sun glasses or perfumes or key chains or coin purses or scarves, luxury brands lure a section of clients who are heavy spenders in the premium brand space and are yet to turn big spenders in the luxury space. These spenders are not sure about the return on investment, or

RoI as we call it in corporate parlance. For them, these low-hanging fruits are not value for money, but they certainly are value for label. So they just pay for the logo and are happy as it remains well within their budget. That way, they are not frivolous, but smart. For them, these spends are a deal. The product may be a key chain or a coin purse, but who cares. Logo rules!

With time, a certain segment of this class realizes the efficacy of the entire experience of luxury shopping, that you pay the premium for not just the product, but the experience as well. So to some it is worth the buck, to others it isn't. Everything is relative.

The ease with which they migrate may differ, but the migration is destined. You are no longer satisfied with a key chain; you need to flaunt a wallet, shoe, handbag, glasses, pens, ties, and the list goes on. This is just stage two. As you climb up the stages, the stickiness increases with the brands. Stage three is when you start using luxury brands regularly and you have completely migrated from super-premium to luxury, even in your articles of daily use to daily wears. You are so used to the luxury shopping experience that you start feeling uneasy and out of place if you shop anywhere else. You are officially a luxury buyer – it's now your lifestyle. And you embark on the big ticket buys. Congratulations! You are now a member of the world of dazzle and no longer a guest. So the LV key chain that used to dazzle you some time back seems relatively less prominent amidst the

Image 3: *A Cartier Pathere ring, a timeless icon for the company, representing what's both predatory and elegant.*

Cartier wallet, Bulgari frame, Bottega Veneta bag, Salvatore Ferragamo shoes, Gucci belt, an LV briefcase, and a Rolex. You are no longer dazzled by these, but you become a luxe yourself who inspires others, just the way a member invites guests to an exclusive high-brow club.

The critical part for the brand remains in handling clients of all stages – from one through three – so that the ever-changing dazzle-quotient remains intact in this galaxy of luxury. This quotient is their bread and butter, no luxury brand should ever forget that.

Let me give you an example of a Cartier store. My friend, the boutique manager, tells me that every client is important, no matter whether he or she is here for a wallet, a watch, a Trinity necklace, or a ring. However, a subtle difference exists in the degree of engagement among all the three segments. Clients in every segment need to feel special, but they must also feel a little left out in terms of the treatment that is meted out to big-ticket buyers. This aspiration element keeps the ball rolling. There is a room in the store that is beautifully decorated with a touch of the history of Cartier and its India connect. It is in this very room where all high-value deals are closed. The special Trinity and Panthere are on display (see Image 3), which are no longer crafted or sold; they are for your eyes only. So for the watch buyer, an entry into that coveted room is an aspiration and that will bring him back. Relativity rules and these brands make big bucks from it.

Now, the mortal crime for any boutique manager or the team is to judge a client by his or her clothes or the proficiency in speaking English. This is a capital mistake as this kind of exclusion will end up shutting the boutique. My friend, who has a great collection of luxury handbags, visited the luxury brand store in torn jeans, a white tee, and flip-flops. To her surprise, the boutique assistant was not properly groomed, which was criminal, and a complete misfit for a luxury boutique. When she asked him to show her a particular bag, he first told her its price and looked at her. She immediately left the store and swore not to visit it again, also abandoning that brand altogether. That was a permanent loss of a loyal, valued client. And in today's connected universe, this brings a lot of bad word-of-mouth as well as social media negative publicity, which is lethal for the reputation of the brand, globally.

This is how a mix of snobbery and inclusiveness can make or break the reputation of your boutique and, thus, the brand. It is all in the soft skills and presence of mind as to how to lure clients. It has nothing to do with the quality or design of the luxury product.

Every brand needs to pay great attention to the human touchpoints at every outlet across the globe to ensure EMOD or every moment operating discipline. The devil lies in the details. Regular training is important to maintain gold standard in customer service. All boutique attendants need to be aware of the product and the stories of craftsmanship that creates an aura around those products. No matter how much a luxury brand spends on advertising and branding, just one attendant can act as a significant dampener. Therefore, it is the responsibility of every boutique manager to ensure that every staff meets that gold standard and only then he or she should be allowed to interact with a client. With time and experience, they will have a sense of the special theory of relativity, but every brand should ensure that gold standard is maintained at all human touchpoints of the customers. Neglecting it can cost the brand its reputation.

Mostly special, but sometimes general – the theory of relativity rules.

Understanding
Price-Sensitive Consumers

"If you can't stop thinking about it...Buy it."

These wise words form the very foundation of luxury shopping in India. So let us take a sneak peek into the minds of these price-sensitive *desi* shoppers. To classify the great Indian luxury consumers is no mean feat. Several attempts have been made over the years. However, consumers have been able to randomly flout most of these classifications. A classic example was when I saw a gentleman driving a Mercedes E-Class towards the CNG counter of the petrol pump. We can't help saving every penny we can, though we have the indomitable urge to show off or flaunt our status with luxury labels. Another example was when I saw a friend, a high-flying executive with an MNC, strapping a limited edition Omega with an Indian leather band because the Omega strap was "very expensive".

Price sensitivity is an all-pervasive characteristic that unites the great Indian luxury consumers. Deep in our hearts we want every purchase to justify its value against the price paid. It can be in the form of luxe factor or flaunt factor or exclusivity factor or envy factor, but there has to be a value for the money. With price sensitivity as the common thread, let us now delve into the classification.

In a Confederation of Indian Industry-Indian Market Research Bureau (CII-IMRB) study on the changing face of luxury in India, they have classified the luxury consumers, in an interesting manner, into experientialists, connoisseurs, flaunters, and aesthetes. So, dear reader, I thought it will be interesting to delve deeper, going beyond this report and studying these classifications more closely.

First, the Experientialists

This genre typically values new and exciting experiences, more than buying products or brands. They lavishly spend on experiences. In their structured lives, they seek a getaway, hence five star hotel stays, fine dining or adventurous/thrilling experiences are their poison. Luxury to them brings images of being suspended in time and space, not having the pressures of daily life and work responsibilities as they enjoy the time away.

An exquisite piece of art or a handcrafted timepiece may also give a similar experience when you are just in a space where you are appreciating the beauty of it. It is a time warp; every time you look at it, you become so mesmerized by the beauty that you forget your meetings and deadlines. The experience is the luxury. It is the dazzle or the luxe.

Personalization of experiences takes luxury to a new level. It is no longer personalization of menus at fine diners for the elite, which would include the name of the customer being printed on the menu. So for an experimentalist, this is value for money. Going forward, these discerning consumers would like to stay in specialty boutique hotels or resorts, luxury spas, or private apartments and villas when on a holiday.

Now let's meet the Connoisseurs

This genre is passionate in certain areas of interest and is mostly well-informed and knowledgeable about it. These could be art, scotch, wine, watches, writing instruments, cigars, horses, not particularly in that order. These connoisseurs get together and appreciate the finer aspects of their passion. They form clubs and meet for quiet appreciation of the finer things in life – it may be a Horology Society of time-keepers, a Wine Club, a Cuban Cigar Club, or a Super Car Club.

This segment revels in enjoying what they appreciate the most. For instance, the Single Malt Club members come together, discuss, study, debate, and share their appreciation and experiences in high spirits (pun intended).

They will spend their time and money in pursuit of the collection of personal passion points. They make the pursuit of their area of passion a mission and pursue it with zest. They will not bat an eyelid before spending a fortune on limited or handcrafted editions, or anything that upholds the spirit of the bygone era.

They are reluctant to place value on brands, unless it stands for exquisite exclusivity. They take pride in their knowledge of esoteric brands that are not widely known. Luxury to them is purely a matter of the level of craftsmanship, the number of man-hours spent, which will determine the quality of the products or services that they buy. Niche, but specialized brands across categories will make their mark with these consumers. They are willing to pay a higher premium, so curated services, that bring such products to them, will be a great gateway to tap into their need for excellence.

The next segment is the life force that drives luxury in India.

Meet the Flaunters

A socialite friend who used to swear by a clutch that she used to take to every party had secretly confessed that she isn't that fond of it, but only carries it for the monogram tag. That's the power of a brand for this genre.

Welcome to the world of flaunters, who tend to value brand name over all other factors. The visibility of the brand name at strategic positions across the product is a big deal for them, as such purchases denote their status in their society. So the brand needs to be aspirational, else, what's the big deal? The newly-rich or new-money classes, especially their younger counterparts, are mostly badge seekers. For them, the brand name is supposedly the biggest status indicator. There is a strong urge to prove to the society that they are also a part of the elitist luxury brand-wagon.

According to a survey, more such consumers were seen in cities like Ludhiana, where they justify the ownership of brands by stating that they are now in a position and thus have a status which makes it *de rigueur*. Interestingly, for this category of consumers, brands are on a continuum. They can show off Zara as daily wear, to Prada on special occasions with élan.

As flaunters move up the societal ladder, the badge value is conferred not only by the brand, but also by the level of difficulty in obtaining the product or service. Dinner reservation at hard-to-get restaurants, Birkin or Kelly bags for which the wait list is over four years, monogrammed and hot-stamped LV bags with their initials, accessories made from exotic leather such of crocodile or snake – the ability to acquire these with relative ease is a reflection of their status.

To tap this segment of consumers, well-known but exclusive services and products are the way forward.

And last but not the least, I present to you the Aesthetes

To this genre, the brand is much less important than the design. Aesthetes are luxury consumers purely because they have arrived at a stage of income due to which they can indulge in their love for design among luxury brands or products. They will shell out a bomb because the object of desire is hand-crafted and not because of the label. They pride themselves for having an eye that picks up the unique and bold in design.

The difference between them and the connoisseur is that the latter has certain passions which they follow with zeal and the quality and craftsmanship are very important. However, for the former category, it is the aesthetic appeal, the look, the intricacies of the design that appeal to their senses. They are also likely to pursue this aesthetic across categories, unlike a connoisseur.

Aesthetes and flaunters are on the opposite ends of the spectrum. While aesthetes are obsessed with design, label or logo comes quite low on the priority list; for flaunters, label or logo comes right on top and design takes a backseat. However, even aesthetes are flaunters in a way. They also flaunt their exquisite designs and feel pride at the snob-quotient, when most people are not even able to understand or appreciate the elegance. They feel exclusive.

To tap aesthetes, luxury brands need to showcase more distinctive and unique designs.

The most intriguing part is that the experientialist consumer may well be an aesthete when it comes to apparel and accessories, while a connoisseur in art may be a flaunter when it comes to automobiles or his home. Indian consumers are yet to reach a stage where their lives are only dominated by luxury brands and they are constantly evolving.

One must always remember that no matter how much you try to classify us Indians, we are a heady mix of all the above and much more than any study could possibly gauge.

Price-sensitivity, rationality, and conservatism still dominate our minds. So while taking decisions, we allocate weightage to the "value for luxury", "value for logo", and "value for money". For the consumer, it is the allocation of weightage to these elements that finally determines a luxury purchase.

There is a saying that if a Greek checks a car, the first thing he will check is the horn. Similarly, if we Indians do that, we will open the conversation with a query on mileage.

Yes, this happens only in India.

Democratization

*"To hope till Hope creates from its own wreak
the thing it contemplates..."*

– Percy Bysshe Shelley, *Prometheus Unbound*

In the mind of Shelley, Prometheus (which is Greek for "forethought") was the embodiment of humanity's hope for a better tomorrow. A tomorrow free from the restrictions of corrupt government, class, religion, or other social distinctions. Prometheus, being the original foreseer, understood that in order for this dream to become reality, people had to free themselves from the hatred that those distinctions often created.

Similarly, in India, luxury has been the birthright of an elite coterie of Maharajas for generations. The Cartiers, the LVs, and the Rolls Royce were an integral part of the lifestyles of the royalty. Branded luxury was the lifestyle of elite India, a term I have coined to best capture this segment of our great nation belonging to the royals, aristocrats, and the blue blood. For centuries, luxury was never meant for the lesser-privileged or the mere mortals.

The democratization of luxury first started in the West, where wealthy businessmen got a taste of luxury. Then it came to India, freeing the nation from its elitist exclusivity. Luxury, like Prometheus, was now unbound, for anyone and everyone who could afford it, irrespective of the colour of their blood. So the New Maharajas soon started flaunting luxury.

Today, even the luxury of royalty or blue blood comes at a price. You might not be a royal by birth, but royal wedding is the latest fad. The opening of palaces for hotels and such elaborate ceremonies is perhaps the biggest step towards democratization of exclusivity of royalty. So, you may proudly dine at Falaknuma Palace's famed dining hall, which can seat a hundred guests at its 108-foot-long table. The chairs are made of carved rosewood with green leather upholstery. The silverware was made of gold and crystal.

Throw in your moolah, and be a Maharaja.

Royalty is in your wallet.

Now there is another very strong category that drives luxury. I call them masses with means – luxury-rich, but asset-poor. This segment is both an opportunity and a threat to the traditional luxury-goods producers. They are more demanding, selective, and care less for brand loyalty than the high net worth individuals, the archetypal consumers of the old luxury. Ever willing to pay high prices, this emerging class, however, expects commensurate quality; old luxury was never so fussy.

So nothing short of the hottest and trendiest designs, which increasingly have to be marketed in creative (and expensive) ways, including product placements on TV sitcoms that can lure them.

Economists feel that this democratization of luxury is eating into the profits of the luxury-goods manufacturers. To maintain quality and the subsequent tightening of their margins that it implies, they must have the capacity and resources to change designs frequently and get new products into the shops rapidly. They need money, discipline, and clout. Design and creativity are the bedrock of any luxury brand. But the access to financial resources and thorough execution that are part of any professional management really come into their own when times are tough. The vulnerability of small trophy companies becomes more obvious during a downturn.

Let's move into a more interesting segment: the masses with limited means. Let me first introduce a term "masstige" to explain this. A portmanteau of the words mass and prestige, masstige has been described as "prestige for the masses". The term was popularized by Michael Silverstein and Neil Fiske in their book *Trading Up* and *Harvard Business Review* article "Luxury for the Masses". Masstige products are defined as "premium but attainable", having two aspects: (1) They are considered luxury or premium products, and (2) They have price points that fill the gap between mid-market and super premium.

Take for instance, in Korea, LV's Speedy 30 handbag has been nicknamed the three-second bag because it feels like you see one every three seconds. As one of the many entry-level products, this has been developed to deliver value for money on a smaller, yet perhaps equally indulgent, taste of the brand narrative. So, entry-level products – accessories, belts, scarves, wallets, small purses, and the likes – of the luxury brands have a clear demand in this segment. They cater to the need of just flaunting the labels.

Luxury brands extend downwards with these low-hanging, seemingly-affordable fruits to whet the appetite of the value-for-label masses.

So, both the Maharaja and the Praja can flaunt the same labels. Yes, it has taken centuries, but democratization of luxury has finally happened.

Democratization has become the great leveller.

Counterfeits

"Would He (God) wear a pinky ring,
Would He drive a fancy car?
Would His wife wear furs and diamonds,
Would His dressin' room have a star?
If He came back tomorrow,
Well there's somethin' I'd like to know
Could ya tell me,
Would Jesus wear a Rolex on
His television show."

– Ray Stevens

Well, that's the flaunt factor that is associated with Rolex. So when my friend Raghavendra flaunted his brand new all gold Rolex Day-Date, I was taken aback for a minute. He comes from a modest background and the watch costs over INR 20 lakhs. This particular rose gold model is something I have always aspired to buy. Someday, I had consoled myself. It has exquisite craftsmanship, the right mix of luxe and panache, and the patented handcrafted movement. I took the watch very carefully and started checking out the dial…old habit. I realized that the unique identification number that is etched in every Rolex, was missing. I knew at once it was a fake, rather a first copy. The quality of steel and its weight was as good as real. The gold was plated and not solid. The movements were recreated by some craftsman in a remote Chinese or Southeast Asian town, definitely not in Geneva. But a great counterfeit, I must say, as it is usually quite difficult to escape my eyes at first glance.

So I asked Raghavendra how much did he shell out? He said ten thousand rupees. He had purchased it from a website selling luxury brands at a crazy discount, like many others which are doing a roaring business across the globe selling counterfeits. I reluctantly told him that it is a first copy, but a good counterfeit. He said, "Of course, I know that. I just wanted you to see how good it was. See, I don't know whether I will ever be able to buy the real one. But this I can experience today. I am happy. Unlike people like you who are experts, how can anyone say that it is a fake? It is automatic, looks the same. Plus, I am happy that I won't have to wait for a lifetime."

His parting words made me think. Is it worth the wait for people with limited means to get something they aspire for but can't afford? Are counterfeits helping democratize luxury?

Snob value is an integral part of luxury. In the core, they are supposed to be exclusive and not available for all. All thanks to this exclusivity, luxury brands are able to charge a premium.

This exclusivity is usually a legacy that you are made a part of. This dazzle can be replicated by a counterfeit and so can be the label, but you can't replicate the exclusivity that the original can offer. The gold-plated watch may shine more than the solid gold one, but this can't give you the legacy of a Rolex or a Patek or a Breguet.

In order to tap the GIMC, or the Great Indian Middle Class, luxury brands are increasingly becoming more inclusive and extending their brand towards those of limited means. They are focusing on masstige. So the focus is only on the label, the monogram. Even a key ring with just an LV monogram will be coveted as one will think that one has become a part of that legacy already. This might also kill the aspiration of spending more and looking beyond the label.

A world-class brand does not attain a certain stature by only marketing or branding. We need to delve deeper and understand what makes it so sought after in the first place. It is the exquisite craftsmanship, the intense labour hours given by masters in some remote hamlet in Venice, the elegant design, the patented movements, the finishing, and the handcrafted creations. These can't be replicated. These can't be low-priced; these must have a premium and these must be exclusive, just like all good things in life.

So the need of the hour is that these brands need to move beyond just focusing on their labels and start popularizing how these labels have become what they are today. It is the responsibility of these luxury brands to make people aware of the difference between a Rolex-patented movement and a first copy, which is available at a fraction of the price. It is the responsibility of these brands to share with its clients, both current and potential, why they are exclusive, and how futile it is to buy a fake, a counterfeit, or a first copy. Although superficially it might seem that the world of counterfeits is democratizing luxury, in reality, it is actually killing the market. The counterfeits are taking you further away from the real world of elegance, luxe, and exclusivity. The man-hours invested, craftsmanship, patented movements, original designs, elegance, all this just can't be replicated. These elements constitute the brand and the logo is valued because of these and not the other way round. Today, in most cases, it is the tail that is wagging the dog.

A rise of counterfeits and first copies is bound to result in a fall in aspirations of the GIMC and it will take away their craving for exclusivity.

Luxury brands surely have a role cut out for them in achieving this desired outcome and in showcasing that all these elements make the logo.

So the real appreciation of the customers should not be constrained to the logo or the monogram.

Luxury is not skin deep!

The Great Indian
Middle Class

*"The upper class desire to remain so, the middle
class wish to overthrow the upper class, and
the lower class want a classless system."*

– George Orwell

In any civil society, class differentiation is a reality. The trick, however, is not to live in a fool's paradise dreaming of a classless society, but to accept and empower every class so that they realise their potential. The middle class has always been the most powerful driving force in India. And luxury is no exception. So, to whom do you think the major luxury brands owe their existence? No, it is not only the New Maharajas or the masses with means, it is the GIMC – The Great Indian Middle Class. In fact, dear New Maharajas, we, the brand custodians, love to say that you are the biggest drivers of luxury. However, deep in our hearts we know that it is the GIMC, that drives the luxury market in this great nation.

If there is one big purchase of a hot stamped monogram LV trunk, then simultaneously, hundreds of monogram belts, monogram small wallet scarves, bracelets, and the likes fly off the shelves. LV might be reaching one New Maharaja's household, may be for the Nth time, but it also reaches hundreds of households of the aspiring Great Indian Middle Class for the first time.

Feeding into the aspiration of millions is masstige. How to keep the aspiration alive still seems to be the biggest challenge. What if the brand loses its exclusivity and elitism in trying to just dip into the mass market? But then again, the raked up moolah from the sheer volume game is also hard to ignore.

To sell or not to sell (to the masses)? A big question that all luxury brands eternally face.

Many, however, have been able to strike a balance with pricing being the key. The entire process has a few elaborate steps. A patient luxury brand manager once explained to me the following:

1. Identify your signature products and add a premium to their price. These are meant to tease the aspirations of the GIMC, who can't afford them. Mostly display the pictures of these signature items and make sure they are always out of stock and fresh stock is on the anvil from Germany or France. The GIMC will keep coming back.

2. Identify special edition, handcrafted pieces that you want the New Maharajas to buy. These should be on display so that they can look and feel it, and then take it home. These have a premium attached due to their exclusivity.

3. And then come the masstige products to satiate the appetite of the GIMC for them to flaunt that logo of the brand they always aspired to buy.

Interestingly, these luxury brands never advertise their masstige products to the masses. This is a precautionary measure to avoid any visible brand dilution. The targeted class, however, advertises and brands these products to their peers, all for free. So a strong brand pull is generated with this segment, the aspiration lives on and grows, much to a luxury brand's advantage.

Shopping malls, in their part, try to woo the GIMC towards luxury and give them its taste. Curators are mixing luxury, super premium, and premium in the same shopping mall. The Palladium in Mumbai or The Quest in Kolkata has a heady mix, all under the same roof.

This aspiration has also led to the creation of a phenomenal market of knock-offs and first copies. Let me brief you on the rationale behind spending hard-earned money on low quality fakes.

Dear readers, it is aspiration at play again. Not always is it possible for GIMC, for example, to buy a scarf for thirty thousand rupees, when with that money he could have bought a piece of jewellery. And what are the chances of that scarf surviving the washing machine or the domestic help's onslaught? At the end of the day, it is a piece of cloth.

This is where the knock-off market comes to the rescue. You get a similar scarf for five hundred rupees and only a trained eye will be able to tell you the difference. If it is torn, replace with another brand for the same price. The same holds true for belts, small leather goods, coin purses, and the likes. The most interesting part is that you can even aim for a big product, a decent copy, at a fraction of the original price that the GIMC would have otherwise never been able to own.

The most-replicated brands are most-aspired brands such as LV and Rolex.

Coming back to the tale of the low-hanging affordable fruits of the luxury tree, the GIMC will go out of their way to own a piece of that brand, sleep with it and dream about the bigger signature pieces in the larger-than-life posters at the boutiques that always tease them.

Luxury lures the GIMC like a seductress.

Seven Ages

"*All the world's a stage,
And all the men and women merely
players.
They have their exits and their
entrances,
And one man in his time plays many
parts,
His acts being seven ages.*"

– William Shakespeare, *As You Like It*

J ust like the seven ages of man described by William Shakespeare in his play *As You Like It*, a luxury brand is also a mere player. It has its exits and entrances, and one brand in its time plays many parts, its acts being seven ages.

Let me take you through these seven stages of a luxury brand – from conception till death and rebirth. Just like a man, a brand also goes through these motions of life, has its share of ups and downs and it also evolves with time and maturity.

1. *The infant*

> *At first the infant,*
> *Mewling and puking in the nurse's arms.*

Conception

This is a time when a luxury brand is conceived and the creator decides on the *raison d'être*. Sometimes a luxury brand is conceived by accident; and at other times, it is meticulously planned.

This is a critical juncture for any creator as this is the story that justifies the birth of the brand. Be it creating a new luxury label from scratch or making the brand an offshoot of another established brand.

When Gucci acquired the house of Yves Saint Laurent (YSL), designer Tom Ford was named creative director of that label as well, displacing Saint Laurent himself as designer of the company's ready-to-wear line. Saint Laurent did not hide his displeasure with this development, openly and regularly criticizing Tom's collections. In April 2004, Tom parted ways with the Gucci group to launch his own label due to creative differences. Tom Ford brand now is a force to reckon with.

Birth

Brands inherently have a gender. Say a Rolex or a Patek Philippe are masculine brands. Its tagline says: "You never actually own a Patek Philippe. You merely take care of it for the next generation," where it is always a father taking care of his son. Whereas brands like Chanel or Dior are feminine.

(a) Determining the brand gender: So the first step is to determine the gender of the brand. This is primarily dependent on the raison d'être. The right questions to ask will be – what is the product, who is the target client, what is the brand aspiration, what is the niche targeted, and the likes. So once these questioned are addressed, you will know the gender of the brand. Based on that, the entire life journey and positioning is planned.

(b) Incubation: If the brand is launched prematurely, it needs to be saved by immediate incubation, just like with babies. The incubation saves the brand and makes it stronger so that it can face the world later. The "parents" or brand custodians realize that the brand is too fragile to withstand competition and so will die prematurely. This forces the custodian to strengthen the brand and make it fit for survival.

2. *The whining schoolboy*

Then, the whining school-boy with his satchel
And shining morning face, creeping like a snail
Unwillingly to school.

And so the brand that is lovingly born slips into the second stage.

(a) The early years: This is the time of doubts, the irritation of failure or the sweetness of initial success and the exposure to criticism. This is the time when the custodian realizes the strengths and the weaknesses or the areas that need nourishment for it to grow.

(b) The teenage/adolescence/puberty: The custodian soon realizes the changes (hormonal) that a brand is undergoing. This is a critical time when you need to be patient, because even a well-thought-through plan may go haywire and this is when the brand starts developing character. This is the most potent time when a brand starts assuming its own characteristics. It is the responsibility of the custodian to take a decision on whether to tame its natural growth and prune it in the direction the custodian desires, or whether it should take its natural course. The decision of a custodian to adapt the product to the nature of the brand has resulted in creation of iconic brands across the globe.

This is a critical judgement call that a custodian, just like a parent, needs to take.

3. The lover

And then the lover,
Sighing like furnace, with a woeful ballad
Made to his mistress' eyebrow.

This is the time of love.

However, the only difference here is that unlike the lover depicted by the poet, a confident young luxury brand falls hopelessly in love with itself. It just sees how beautiful it is and keeps admiring the story of its birth and growth. This is a time when "Brand Ego" takes birth.

4. A soldier

Then, a soldier,
Full of strange oaths, and bearded like the pard,
Jealous in honour, sudden, and quick in quarrel,
Seeking the bubble reputation
Even in the cannon's mouth.

The brand now fights to upkeep its honour.

This is dedicated to the facets of Brand Ego. "A car that runs of reputation" is one such example. Ego creates brands, makes them reach heights that they could have never reached with humility.

It is the ego and arrogance that a brand exudes, using prohibitive pricing to crowd out clients, to make it aspirational. For example, Rolex sells legacy, a life of greatness, a masculine ego that craves for being distinguished.

This is a time when the brand, just like a soldier, is fighting a relentless war to establish its honour and respect, protecting its ego. This is the time when the custodian needs to ensure that the brand ego doesn't become the reason for its fall. So adding the right measure of arrogance is the responsibility of the custodian.

5. The justice

And then, the justice,
In fair round belly, with a good capon lined,
With eyes severe, and beard of formal cut,
Full of wise saws, and modern instances,
And so he plays his part.

The brand now matures to understand its clientele.

Ego grows and so does wisdom as the brand matures. The luxury brand now has more clarity of its clients and its target group, and even about its strengths and weaknesses. It knows about its competition too. This is the time of maturity. This is the time of the brand ego to take on a larger role. This is the time of arrogance. And this is the time for the custodian to be judicious about the synergy between the product, the brand, and the ego.

6.   *Into lean and slippered pantaloon*

The sixth age shifts
Into the lean and slippered pantaloon,
With spectacles on nose and pouch on side,
His youthful hose, well saved, a world too wide
For his shrunk shank, and his big manly voice,
Turning again toward childish treble, pipes
And whistles in his sound.

This is a time when the brand starts to show signs of fading. The idea that the brand is nearing death looms large. So the custodian or the parent looks at ways to save the brand or rebuild the brand, or even at the birth of a new brand.

The brand starts to reinvent itself. The brand understands that its target has shifted and if it does not evolve, it will perish. This is a time when very traditional and conservative brands such as a Rolls Royce or a Breguet or a Mont Blanc recognize the immense potential of the youth and remodels its brand to create sporty and more youthful versions of their traditional bestselling products.

However, all these established brands also run the risk of alienating its existing loyal customer base in the process of creating a new identity. This is a risk that no brand can ever avoid. The trick is to know the right time to take the plunge before it is too late to even re-invent its identity.

7. Second childishness

Last scene of all,
That ends this strange eventful history,
Is second childishness and mere oblivion,
Sans teeth, sans eyes, sans taste, sans everything.

This is the stage of the death of the old brand. However, unlike man, the brand can see a new birth – the second life of the brand. In its new avatar, the brand can either metamorphose itself into an altogether different identity, or it can still retain the legacy of its earlier form, like a chip of the old block.

"I'm like a phoenix. I rise from the ashes."

Ego-centric

*"This town is a make you town
Or a break you town and bring you down
town..."*

– Frank Sinatra (This Town)

Every time I hear this wonderful song by the great Frank Sinatra, I am reminded of a three-letter word that has the same power: *Ego*.

Ego can make you or break you. Like John Lennon, you might feel like saying: "Part of me suspects that I'm a loser, and the other part of me thinks I'm God Almighty." Like people, even brands need to be careful in dealing with ego.

Not humility but ego creates brands, makes them reach the stars. As Sherlock Holmes once said, "My dear Watson, I cannot agree with those who rank modesty among the virtues".

But false ego can put you down and crush you. So your brand has to be worth it. Rolls Royce once run an ad where the car did not have a fuel tank. The arrogant tagline, as I had mentioned earlier, said: "A car that runs on reputation". (See page 72.)

For a luxury brand, being humble never pays, it's all about being special or exclusive. The brand should be able to dazzle or luxe, to stand out in the crowd. This razzle-dazzle industry thrives on ego.

The marketer tries to sell an exclusivity quotient, so when you flaunt a particular label, you at least notionally belong to an exclusive club, like a Lamborghini Club. "Money can't buy happiness. But, somehow, it is more comfortable to cry in a Lamborghini than on a bicycle". Lamborghini Gallardo slogan quite captures the ethos (see Image 4).

Image 4: *"Money can't buy happiness. But, somehow, it is more comfortable to cry in a Lamborghini than on a bicycle."*

The arrogance that comes from prohibitive pricing to crowd out clients makes a brand aspirational. When Rolex says "Live for greatness", it is not talking about the product, or the patented perpetual movement, or the oyster casing, or the brilliant design…it is talking about an aspiration. You are entering the league of greats like John F. Kennedy or of Martin Luther King Jr and the likes. Being a masculine brand always, Rolex has been able to develop and nurture male ego over decades. This has proved instrumental for the company's success and it is still revelling in that glory. In a way, the brand is selling legacy, a life of greatness, a masculine ego that stands distinguished.

Another example is LV. "There are journeys that turn into legends". When LV used this tagline for Sean Connery during its core values campaign, it was not selling the classic keep-all travel bag. It was selling a story of a great legendary travel, and that too with a legend.

The art is in not only selling the inclusion, but more so selling the exclusion.

India's noted graphic novelist and my friend Sarnath Banerjee (author of *Corridor* and *All Quiet in Vikaspuri*) has captured the essence of this "exclusion principle in a story", albeit in his own comic panache. There are customers who walk in and quickly check a few models and close the buy. However, there are others who come down to check out an expensive car like a Rolls Royce or a Jaguar, but are not sure whether it is worth that premium. This kind is more for an economical car with a better mileage but the legacy factor still haunts them. The car salesman instead of hard selling, brilliantly captures this dilemma and thereby hangs a tale. The salesman very cleverly says that these luxury cars are not for "people like you and I" who will prefer more value for their money and not invest in such "esoteric and intangible" notions of legacy. Needless to say, after four-five such examples of "people like you and I", the deal is closed. The legacy wins again and so does the aspiration.

Ironically, we all are in the same queue, waiting eagerly to be treated as special. The "exclusion principle" works like magic.

Stroking the aspiration to be a part of legacy is a strategy that luxury brands use in tapping into the potential customers who have the money, but are not convinced about the value for their buck that such a luxury product will bring to their lives. They are, however, also intrigued at the differential treatment doled out to them by the boutique managers for not being a part of its existing esteem clientele. The potential clients are never ignored, but they are subtly sent the message that "you also can become a part of this elite treatment and legacy if you use your cash or card a little more generously". This exclusion principle makes these clients with means feel intrigued and dejected. In comes "greatness" and "legacy" to the rescue. The deal then is no more only value for money, but also "totally worth it".

And "for people like you and I", who do not have the means, keep aspiring and writing about the legacy.

Just a swipe, and the legacy is yours.

Click Click

"A fake is a fake is a fake is a fake."

A little modification of a famous quote by Gertrude Stein will give you the essence of this chapter. Just the way a rose in any other name remains a rose, a fake in any expensive veil – online or offline – remains a fake. Allow me to quote my former boss Mr Sanjiv Goenka, Chairman of RP-SG group: "Mahul has a great love for luxury watches and had almost twisted my wrist a couple of times to check my watch." SG knows I am crazy about watches, so he is sweet enough to forgive me and let me indulge, even with his IWC or Breguet. Similarly, Mr TV Narendran, Managing Director, India and SE Asia, Tata Steel, too, very kindly, lets me admire his black Chopard while I narrate to him the details of the craftsmanship of the watch. Unfortunately, I ended up breaking the heart of a very close friend with this habit. She was sporting a Cartier gold watch. I did the same thing with her and, to my shock, realised it was a first copy. She very confidently told me it isn't as there was a certification of authenticity given by the company and the portal that she bought it from. The price she had shelled out was just a fraction of the original price, but it was significantly more than that of a first copy. The news that she has been duped by an e-commerce firm broke her heart.

On Facebook, you might encounter a page where they are selling luxury products at a tempting discount of 70 or 80% all-round the year. The products range from shoes to watches to handbags of the luxury brands like Rolex, LV,

Gucci, Mont Blanc, and what have you! Tempting! So I decided to check them out. To my utter dismay, I found that these products were counterfeits. And some were not even on the catalogues of the brands. These counterfeit versions were a result of overflow of creative juices of the craftsman. To an untrained eye, it will lure you and you will fall into its trap, just like my friend did. I was happy when I came to know that LVMH and Mont Blanc have noticed as well and have filed a lawsuit against a Chandigarh-based e-commerce firm in Delhi High Court for duping people.

The counterfeit market statistics

Dear Reader, let me give you a sense of the size of the market with some statistics. Growing at a compounded annual growth rate of almost 40-45%, the counterfeit luxury products market in India is likely to more than double to INR 5,600 crore from the current level of about INR 2,500 crore.

A reason why the market of luxury fakes is growing at such a fast pace is the advent of e-commerce platforms selling them at lucrative prices. Web shopping portals account for over 25% of the fake luxury goods market in India. For instance, first copies of these luxury brands are easily available on ***offer.com, an online portal, within a week of official launch of the original collection. Even other platforms like Qui** and O** offer replicas. While

Qui** has a replica Hermes belt for Rs 350, Watch**.com or the Facebook page watchmania****** stocks first copies of around twenty brands, including TAG Heuer, Omega, Rado, Patek Phillipe, Chopard, and Bulgari. These are just a few of the numerous options to choose from and all from the comfort of your home with a doorstep delivery and cash-on-delivery provision.

The size of counterfeit luxury industry in India is currently about 5% of the overall market size of India's luxury industry, which currently is worth over $14 billion. With a share of about 7%, fake luxury products account for over $22 billion of the global luxury industry worth about $320 billion.

With technological advances and sophisticated new ways to reach consumers, the business of producing luxury counterfeits is expanding rapidly.

Historically, luxury counterfeits were often shipped in large cargo containers and passed through numerous middlemen before reaching the final consumers. However, now counterfeit sellers set up online presence on auction or marketplace sites and ship luxury counterfeits directly to consumers. They also use the internet and social media tools to generate web traffic and to divert consumers to rogue e-commerce websites selling their goods which often have the same look and feel as the brand owner's site. Compared to the purchase of a fake handbag on the street, the purchase of a bag online makes it harder for a consumer to tell whether the product is genuine. An online advertisement by these portals for a Gucci bag could show a photo of a genuine Gucci bag, but the purchaser would actually receive a fake one. The counterfeit seller may create pseudo product reviews, blog entries, and rogue social media profiles to enhance its legitimacy. Susceptible consumers can fall for this fake content easily.

According to a report by Anna Maria Lagerqvist and Hanna Bruck in Valea International, in 2009 Eurobarometer statistics, 22% of European Union citizens have unknowingly bought counterfeit goods. As shopping online is considered entirely legitimate, online counterfeit products may attract consumers who would never purchase a LV handbag in a dark alley. The internet creates a situation where the marketplaces for counterfeit products and for the genuine article are suddenly the same.

Further, online shops give buyers a sense of anonymity and impunity. Given the seemingly boundless scope of the internet, luxury brand owners come across anonymous online counterfeit sellers every day.

Over 80% of the imitation luxury products being sold in India come from China and most of these consist of handbags, watches, shoes, clothes, hats, sunglasses, perfumes, and jewellery, according to a report by The Associated Chambers of Commerce and Industry in India (ASSOCHAM).

According to a 2012 report on the luxury retail market by Cognizant, brands such as Kate Spade and LV typically hire private investigators to find where counterfeits are sold. On the other hand, Indian stores like Kitsch, offering high-end labels, inform the head offices of brands when they come to know about an individual or a store selling copies.

Quality difference among fakes

There is a world of difference between a replica, first copy, and fake. There are huge qualitative differences between counterfeits. In my recent visit to Bangkok, I was exploring the counterfeit market. The two brands that dominate the world of replicas are Rolex and LV.

Take for example a Rolex watch. I was checking out a Rolex all gold Day-Date counterfeit across quality standards. The difference in prices between a first copy and a fake is 75%. The first copy was heavier, the steel quality was superior, the gold plating was much neat and there was even an identification number! While the fakes even had models that never made it to the catalogues of Rolex, the first copies were sold with the original catalogue by their side. Very impressive indeed!

Similarly with the replicas of LV. Even to a trained eye, the monogram or Damier Ebene will be hard to decipher.

On the online platform however, the fakes dominate. The first copies and replicas (in the true sense) can't make a mark as on the online platform, no customer will be ready to pay the premium. While a Rolex fake may be available at INR 5,999, a first copy will cost at least double that, for differences that are not visible to untrained eyes, especially while comparing online.

However, some counterfeit e-commerce sites take a contrarian view. They think that selling first copies at a higher price will be able to make them more credible as the prices are double compared with replicas on the other sites. Moreover, as the quality is far better, they believe they will get repeat customers.

In defence of counterfeits

At times I ask myself whether these brands have a legitimate justification for charging such a prohibitive premium for their merchandise.

A few counterfeit watch dealers have showed me copies of watches with complicated movement and how their watchmen were able to replicate to the very details of the original. The cost of their labour? Well, just a fraction of the cost of the labour of a legitimate watchmaker with a luxury brand. When I see the detailing, my heart goes out to them, but not to the dealers.

The counterfeit market is eating into not only the pie of the luxury brands but also into the pie of the premium brands. Say if someone can afford a Tissot, aspires to wear an Omega Seamaster, and gets a Rolex first copy at INR

5,999 online! Tissot and Omega both lose the battle, for no fault of theirs.

From the buyer's perspective, understand this: the difference between the cost of making a Gucci or LV handbag and the MRP is significant, and that is the brand value. The buyer is getting a cheap quality leather handbag but along with that the "perceived brand quotient" in a fake at an affordable price and that too at their doorsteps.

Luxury (counterfeit) is just a click away.

Experiential Luxury

"Experience is not what happens to a man; it is what a man does with what happens to him."

– Aldous Huxley

L uxe is a purely experiential phenomenon as it is heavily dependent on how your senses perceive something. If your senses feel dazzled, you are convinced to shell out that premium for a luxury brand.

As you now know, e-commerce is widely used by firms for selling luxury counterfeits online, even with authentication certificates. And unfortunately, they are doing well, barring a few legal hassles from luxury brands when they are caught. There are buyers as it is convenient to buy counterfeits online and also there are users who are not aware that these are replicas or first copies. They are just lured by 70-80% discount that they are offered.

However, this chapter will deal with a scenario wherein e-commerce websites are selling genuine luxury goods and not counterfeits. Therefore, we are taking the discount card off the table. Now, let us look into the inherent incoherence at the core of the marriage between e-commerce and luxury and why it is destined for a divorce or a failure. But let us first look into these two individually.

E-commerce or e-retail has been a game-changer. The valuation game in which these biggies have entered into is a completely new premise for any business. Their valuation is increasing at the cost of making losses. But the million dollar question is – how are they sustaining it? They are sustaining it because of the valuation game that will fetch them a buyer with very deep pockets. The buyer will look into the transactional value and the spectrum of offerings, so the focus is that and not profit. It is a great joyride for us consumers as the unrealistic discounts offered at the cost of company money may be funded by a private equity fund in China.

But as all good things come to an end, the risk of the bubble bursting is imminent. Business models can't run on losses. Period. Cracks are already becoming visible.

E-commerce has transformed the way we shop. Even a few years back, we couldn't even fathom buying clothes or shoes without trying them on, but today it has become the norm. It has penetrated our lives like mobile phones have. Shopping has never been this convenient as well as cost-effective.

The reason behind the success of e-commerce in India is our love for price-sensitivity. We love discounts, we love value for our money. The entire machinery of e-commerce or e-retail runs on unrealistic deals and discounts.

And this is where the meeting of hearts between e-commerce and luxury doesn't happen. So let us understand the premises on which luxury buying is based in India.

The entire shopping experience wherein you try a great pair of shoes or a lovely shirt and look at the mirror and then decide whether you should buy it or try another one can't ever be replicated by an image of the same product, even with a 360 degree view. It is next to impossible to excite and convince our senses via a laptop, tab, or mobile screen.

And that is why the e-commerce companies try the same strategy of heavy discounts that they try for premium products. Unfortunately, this story of crazy discounts opens another can of worms – the world of luxury counterfeits that are sold online.

My friend very recently sought my advice for buying an Omega through a e-commerce website which was offering a discount of 40%. But Omega was not offering that discount at any of its retail outlets. Although the price was realistic, I advised her against it as you will never know for sure, without the manufacturer's warranty, in this case Omega, whether it is an original or a counterfeit.

When you are paying a hefty premium for a luxury purchase, you are paying for the experience. You walk into a luxury boutique, the way you are greeted with a smile and offered a special treatment from the word go, it is bound to make you feel good and special. The boutique manager will make you feel that you are almost on the verge of entering an exclusive and elite club with an amazing history and legacy – it is just a purchase away. Then your senses, which are already feeling special, actually experience that the goods feel more special. For example, the latest Omega watch that James Bond is sporting in *Spectre* is on your wrist. How can you not feel elated? You have already "bonded" with that timepiece. You just know this is the one. The boutique manager keeps pampering you, sometimes even with a glass of Champagne. So finally when you make the payment, it feels so justified and incidentally also "value for money". You will revel in that Bond moment.

The entire ambience, the entire experience cannot be created online by any e-commerce company, not even via simulation. No matter how much convenience or best deals you are offered, luxury shopping cannot happen without experience. It is not worth the money for the buyer and no amount of discount can replicate that experience.

So the value for money as understood by a customer shopping for clothes or shoes from an e-commerce website is not the same in case of luxury shopping online. In the former, it is just the hefty discounts that do the trick, but in the latter, it is the experiential worth of money.

No wonder the marriage between e-commerce and luxury is destined for failure.

You just can't experience luxe online.

Strategic Moves-I

"The basic approach of positioning is not to create something new and different, but to manipulate what's already in the mind, to retie the connections that already exist."

– Al Ries and Jack Trout,
Positioning: The Battle for your Mind

S trategic positioning is a pure play mind game. If you go by the classical definition, positioning is a marketing strategy that aims to make a brand occupy a distinct position, relative to competing brands, in the mind of the customer. The above quote by Al Ries and Jack Trout in their book *Positioning: The Battle for your Mind* echoes the classical approach to brand positioning, but primarily is referring to positioning of an existing brand and not a brand that wants to make an entry.

So let us understand the phases of this extraordinary make-or-break tool.

When you conceive of launching a brand in the luxury space, the first step is to study the market. A study of the existing players and your competition, and how they have positioned themselves all this while will give you a fair idea of the positioning that you are looking at.

Strategically, if the incumbent brand has a strong recall then it is prudent to find a new positioning for your brand. In case the existing brand is new, you may even try to replace its positioning.

For example, when the incumbent is positioning itself as a brand with heritage and legacy, you might consider positioning your brand as youthful or rather "cool". Yes, a luxury brand can be positioned as "a cool brand". The greatest advantage of such a brand positioning is that it appeals not only to the young people who can afford it, but also to the young-at-heart who want to sport a brand that is "cool", sporty, and youthful.

Tom Ford is such a brand that has appealed to the youthfulness of the clients. And small wonder, not only youth but also clients from more senior demography, even James Bond, have been loyal to Tom Ford brand. Other top designers like Michael Kors and Marc Jacobs have also made a niche for themselves by appealing to the youthfulness and vibrancy of their clients with their labels.

So while conceiving a luxury brand, the positioning will make or break it.

Now let us examine the positioning or rather re-positioning of an existing luxury brand. When I saw Rolls Royce launching a Wraith, I wondered for a while, "How will this sporty car fit into the RR family, beside Phantom and Ghost?" (See Image 5.) The reason is simple. Rolls Royce doesn't want to confine its positioning to a brand of legacy and heritage that is associated with a certain level of power and seniority. A similar example is LV. Louis Vuitton's brand ambassadors have classically been Bono, Angelina Jolie, and Sean Connery. This was essentially the "core values" campaign about how "a single journey can change your life". The idea was to create aspiration for the youth and create a pull for both the young and the not-so-young. However, they realized that it is time to tap into the market they were missing out on. So, the then creative director Marc Jacobs designed the Damier series of designs to attract youth and to reposition LV brand as youthful.

Image 5: *"A car that runs on reputation": Rolls Royce Phantom.*

Now let us discuss the final facet or rather a dilemma that every luxury brand faces – a choice between exclusivity and dilution. When a brand is snob and has priced itself at such a level that it is alienating a greater part of the potential clients, it is gaining exclusivity. It remains an aspiration. People who can't afford, resolve to buying first copies and fakes. However, some other brands make the pricing competitive to include a large pool of clients who are ready to invest significantly on a first copy. So they are drawing that money and making luxury brands affordable. Handling the masstige segment is the toughest for any brand manager. To what extent can you dilute your brand to gain volume and tap into the wide pool of counterfeit buyers and provide customers with originals that they can afford? It can be a key chain or a coin purse or a wallet or a belt – it is all about flaunting the label, that too original. The pride associated with it is enormous, so the aspiration to buy the bigger product only grows and the brands get a new set of wider client pool.

The selling point is simple: the client takes greater pride in owning an original coin purse from the glamorous boutique than owning a first copy duffle bag from a not-so-glamorous store or from some e-commerce website.

The only risk is brand dilution, which might position the brand away from exclusivity and result in loss of loyal big-ticket clients who want to claim exclusive rights to "luxe".

The efficacy of the job of a brand custodian lies in his or her power of knowledge of the brand when it comes to positioning a new luxury brand or repositioning an existing brand, or even handling the exclusivity versus dilution debate. The more you know your brand, the better you can decide on its positioning. The brand custodian will only be able to do justice if he or she not only has the knowledge of the brand but also of the entire ecosystem, which includes competitors, mindset of target customers, their purchasing power, market demand, geography, as well as demography.

In your quest, the strategic positioning of the mast will ensure a smooth sail.

Strategic Moves-II

"A horse, a horse! My kingdom for a horse!"

– William Shakespeare, *Richard III*

Well, that's luxury marketing opportunity the bard William Shakespeare has spelt out for you in his play *Richard III*. It is the game of pure play demand of luxe-addiction and constrained supply in the name of limited-edition or handcrafted-edition.

The first step is in understanding the very basic difference between marketing of luxury vis-à-vis non-luxury brands.

A marketer needs to understand that straightforward cost-effectiveness or discount card is off the table. You have to sell the dazzle card, not the value-for-money card (not upfront, it will come in a very different format much later in the play).

So luxe is your USP, the Unique Selling Proposition.

The second step is to sell the story – a tale of aspiration, a tale that you will want the buyer to crave to be a part of. This story will justify the premium you are charging. This needs to be a story of legacy, of historical stature, and of aspiration.

The third step is in convincing the client that this is the only chance, the only window of opportunity to become part of that legacy. The object – be it a watch (say a Rolex) or a writing instrument (Montblanc) or a trunk (LV) or a car (Rolls Royce) – will make the client a part of that proud history. So the strategy is that even after listening to the history, if the client is still is not convinced, convince the person that it would be a big mistake to lose this opportunity of a lifetime.

The key(words) that usually help the client make up his mind are – handcrafted, limited edition, special edition, exclusive, hand-picked, and exquisite craftsmanship in some remote hamlet in Venice. It directly opens your executive brain. Your pupils dilate and you feel an increasing craving for it. As the story progresses, it slowly draws you in. But then, suddenly, comes the price tag.

The mindset of a typical Indian buyer seldom goes beyond "value-for-money". So you have to address that at the same level. But never in the first step; only after the story is sold. The premium charged is complete value for money because the legacy is priceless. The moment the client is sold on the value, proposition the deal is sealed.

Now let us look into the steps that need to be taken for strategic marketing of new brands which want to make a mark in the luxury space.

First, dear marketeer, define the brand aspiration, the strategic objective. For example, ten years down the line, you want to become the most-sought after watch brand among men in the age-group of 30-45 years at a certain price point in China. So the objective needs to be very specific and spelt out – period, geography, target audience, price point, and the likes.

Second, weave a story – a story of legacy, of exquisite craftsmanship. A story that justifies the raison d'erte in the luxury brand space.

The third step is to understand and take stock of the initial conditions in the minutest details – what is the current positioning, which is the current target group, what is the current price point, which is the geography currently present in, and what's the position vis-à-vis competition.

This will give you clarity on the distance you have to traverse to reach your strategic objective.

The fourth step is to define in every minute detail the final conditions. This will flesh out the brand aspiration into specific targets. This will capture all the conditions that will enable attaining the strategic objective. Say, elimination of current market leader in that geography, dominating a certain geography, top of the mind recall among men in a specific age bracket, and the likes. This will help flesh out the final results that you want to achieve for reaching the strategic objective.

The fifth and most crucial step is to formulate action points which will help map the starting point to the end points. These action points will show how to bridge the gap between the initial "have-nots" and the final "haves". This mapping will tell you how over the years, one year at a time, you will slowly reach your objective of brand aspiration. Study the model of competition and understand the modalities on how marketing should be done differently, what is the selling point, what is the story, and the likes.

These action points are basically strategic marketing activities put together in the marketing plan.

Dear marketeer, you should always remember: the story is priceless.

A marketeer's quick guide for creating a strategic marketing or branding objective is as follows:

1. First, identify the overall strategic marketing objective and what is currently being done (under initial conditions).

2. Mention the current strategic approach.

3. Show the external environment which impacts and influences the marketing or branding efforts – this should have data and trends. Mention your sources of information. In elements of external analysis, include the social and political forces at play – consumer behaviour, regulations, and policies. Also capture what marketing or branding activities are pursued by competitors.

4. Show the internal environment which impacts and influences the marketing or branding efforts – this should have data and trends on your internal performance. In elements of internal analysis, include customer feedback, cost analysis, and trend requirements.

5. The output for external analysis should be "opportunities" and "threats" for branding.

6. The output for internal analysis should be "strengths" and "weaknesses" for branding.

7. The new strategic objectives should come out of the SWOT.

Now do the mapping and chart the action plan with timelines.

Managing Reputation

"You can't build a reputation on
what you are going to do."

– Henry Ford

R eputation is born with the birth of a brand. Just like the brand itself, the reputation needs to be nurtured and, more importantly, protected. Reputation can't be built on what you are promising to deliver or achieve; it is only dependent on the promises that you keep, on whether you walk the talk.

It takes years, even decades, to build the reputation of a luxury brand and just moments to ruin it as the Oracle of Omaha Warren Buffett had once rightly said. So a brand custodian's primary responsibility along with building the brand is to protect and build on the reputation.

With luxury brands, as these are not personality-dependent, reputation management is primarily managing the reputation of the product or service in the eyes of the customers. A brand custodian needs to always remember that the customer is at the centre.

With social media becoming all-powerful, this is a medium that needs to be kept under strict observation. One tweet by a happy customer can be leveraged for building reputation, while on the other hand, one tweet by an unhappy customer can snowball into a reputation disaster in no time, even for the biggest of the brands. Not very long back, a huge brand, which is primarily into trunks and other leather/canvas goods, had released an ad where it showed that the trunks were handmade. The reality was different. The trunks were machine-made and only a small part of the stitching process was manual. This truth after it was exposed on social media dented the reputation of the brand significantly.

So, the first lesson is to know that honesty is the best policy. A brand is basically the sum of its virtues and its reputation is sum of how much it is living up to those virtues. So if the brand is living up to its brand promise, then it is able to not only protect but also build its reputation.

A brand has promises to keep. And customer satisfaction is the biggest promise. Ensuring that a customer is satisfied with the promises made by the luxury brand is the biggest responsibility of the brand custodian, besides building the brand. As every touchpoint of the brand is responsible for making the brand, they can also ruin the reputation in no time. Just one instance of rude behaviour by a boutique assistant can generate apathy in the mind of the customers and social media can add momentum, mass, and voices to this grievance. So, it is literally a walk on the tightrope. Every element of the brand has to ensure that only the best is delivered to the customer as they are the king.

Luxe is experiential. So the premium that a brand charges for the luxe is largely dependent on the experience of the customer. Then, one instance of rude behaviour or even a slight reluctance to serve can break it to pieces.

So, reputation management for a luxury brand comprises three aspects – living up to the brand promises, living up to the brand virtues, and keeping customers at the centre of its universe.

Measuring Luxe

"If you can't dazzle them with brilliance,
baffle them with bull."

– W.C. Fields

L uxury is all about the dazzle, and dazzle is all about perception. And a brand custodian really can't take the route with the bull as Fields suggested as an alternative. So, there is no universal LQ – Luxe Quotient, or the luxe factor – as I would like to name them. It all depends on the sample that you choose to determine the "LQ" or "luxe factor" of a luxury brand.

The LQ is a unique measure for capturing the longing and desire for a luxury brand. It has the ability to capture the relative dazzle factor between two or more comparable brands from the perspective of a customer. So if we choose two brands of watches in a sample, say Rolex and Omega, "LQ" will tell you which one is more dazzling (for the same customer) in the chosen sample. That will determine a higher LQ for that brand for you. This classification can be made even for one customer segment, say for experientialists or connoisseurs or flaunters or aesthetes. So basically a segment is chosen and brands are compared. The higher desirability for that segment of customer for one brand means LQ is higher, say for Rolex versus Omega for the segment of flaunters.

You can also take a weighted average among all four categories of customers to understand the LQ of one brand compared with another.

Dear reader, you might recall my apple to apple comparison earlier. My dazzle with a Cartier ring or a LV sling just seem very lacklustre when we look at the Maharaja of Patiala's Cartier crown with 234.69 carat De Beers diamond or Maharaja of Jammu & Kashmir's customized thirty LV trunks. This difference in dazzle is captured by luxe factor.

This is from the perspective of the brand towards the customer. So it will be the same brand and different customers and their dazzle factors. For LV, which is looking at two customers, say yours truly and Maharaja of Jammu & Kashmir, I have a higher luxe factor for LV compared with the Maharaja. For me, the dazzle factor for the same brand is much higher. Similarly, for Cartier, my luxe factor for it is higher than that of the Maharaja of Patiala.

The degree of dazzle is a crucial enabler that every luxury brand needs to understand very clearly.

As discussed earlier, when you want to own a piece of luxury, you are well aware of the premium that you will have to pay. If you are price sensitive, then this will be a very difficult proposition, justifying the premium. So the best way to justify the premium charged is through the value for money route. So let us first look at the routes through which a luxury product can be a great value for money.

The premium is charged because by purchasing that product, you will be a part of an elite and exclusive club, you will be part of the legacy of that brand. So you are also paying to be a part of the history, of the legendary brand story.

Then comes the experience. When you are paying a heavy premium for a luxury purchase, you are paying for the experience.

However, above all this are the factors that actually draw you to make the purchase: the LQ and the luxe factor. These measures the extent to which the product mesmerizes you, draws you. The LQ and luxe factor are simply the razzle-dazzle factors. The story that is weaved around the brand, the legacy that is associated with the brand, and the experiential gratification that is attached to the brand all contribute towards creating this luxe and increasing this desirability.

This desirability determines the extent to which you will be able to exert yourself to indulge in the luxury brand. The craving, the eagerness, the longing, the desire, all are captured here.

How much you will be dazzled is very personal, so there isn't any universal degree of LQ or luxe factor for any particular brand. It depends on the sample chosen. Thus, while comparing, the sample is kept the same and the LQ determines which brand is more dazzling and more desired. The luxe factor shows it from the brand's perspective. i.e. which customer has more desirability for that particular brand.

The LQ and luxe factor are great tools that brands across the globe must use to study the dazzle of their brand and customer's desirability and then they can rework their brand story accordingly to reach their desired LQ or luxe factor.

The Quantum of Luxury matters.

The Dark Side

"I'll see you on the dark side of the moon."

– Pink Floyd

All this while, I have talked about dazzle and its various facets, including measures. This chapter will deal with the other side of dazzle or luxe. Its dark side, a side that is not much talked about.

Luxury has always, since the days of royalty, been used as a tool for establishing class difference. Luxury has played a major role in re-instating the "great divide" between the rich and the poor.

Flaunting luxury has been the greatest passion of the Maharajas, as well as their royal aspirants or loyalists, like the zamindars.

Luxury has been a great tool for one-upmanship and some secret fetishes since ages. This is a very heavily guarded side that all luxury retailers are silent about. However, these were a chunk of their revenues then and so the demand was supplied generously. At that time, there used to be dealers, mostly European traders, of these luxury items who primarily used to make their living from the generous commissions of the Maharajas and zamindars. Thereby hangs a lesson for retailers and brand custodians.

I will share a few such instances to give you the feel of the other side of luxury that took place in Bengal in the nineteenth and early twentieth centuries. *Hootum Panchar Naksha* or *The Observant Owl: Hootum's Vignettes of Nineteenth-century Calcutta*, by Kaliprasanna Sinha is a great chronicle for such dark secrets prevalent during those days. The biggest and most common exhibition of luxury was with the Nautch girls. The one-upmanship was so severe that in most of the cases it led to the downfall of the zamindari itself.

My friend and graphic novelist Sarnath Banerjee, however, has shared a few other stories of more interesting and uncommon forms of dark luxe in his own rendition of the Owl's classic tale. A certain sloshed zamindar accidentally hit a chandelier with his cane, knocking it off the ceiling. It fell with a terrific crash. He was so mesmerized with the tinkling of breaking glass that he broke all the glass within his reach that night. Every piece of glass was imported from Belgium and the Chandelier would have cost a fortune, even then. He had a moment of "enlightenment" and realized the more expensive the glass, the sweeter the sound.

Then began a long career of importing expensive glass from the biggest international brands from all over the world, aided by a European trader. A few examples were sixteenth century goblet from Prague, Ming dynasty bone China, Belgian mirrors, French wine glasses, and crystal paper weights from the Austro-Hungarian empire.

He made it a private hobby to break these and listen to their "music". And sometimes he made a grand spectacle of his passion. Once he laid out four giant-sized Belgian mirrors on the street and had his brother's carriage run over them. Small wonder, his debt rose astronomically and he died a destitute.

Another story that Sarnath had shared in his book was the competition between two zamindars or babus on how expensive their open-top phaetons (horse carriages, modern-day convertibles) were. So they started adding horses. This competition rose to a level where one of them replaced the horses with zebra. This story is not uncommon when we see the competition among the Richie Rich to showcase their imported two- and four-wheeled "beauties" unabashedly.

One-upmanship has been a great driver for luxury brands since ages.

Like modern-day elite car manufacturers, these makers of phaetons were able to brand them as exclusive, giving certain features to make them aspirational.

Be it on the dark side or the brighter side, branding has played a crucial role in luxury retailing. Even way back in time, why do you think the Maharaja of Patiala wanted Cartier to design his necklace and not any other jeweller? Why even did the Nizam buy Harley Davidson for his personal postmen and not any other motorcycle brand? (See Image 6.) Why did the Maharaja of Kashmir asked LV to customize trunks? All these brands were able to first establish an aspiration quotient. That would have taken years, but they were patient and gave all the time to the custodian for establishing and maturing the brand. And that is the only reason why these brands have stood the test of time. As luxury or luxe is all about perception, the value

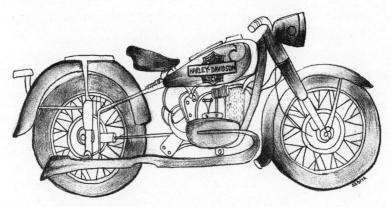

Image 6: *50 Harley Davidsons were procured by a Nizam for his postmen.*

of the brand will determine how much premium you are willing to shell out to own that dazzle.

Every luxury brand needs to first focus on the measures that I had created – luxe factor, LQ, and aspiration quotient. The only endeavour should be to increase them. It is only after your brand has attained a certain level in these measures compared to your competition that you will know that your premium will be accepted by the consumers.

So don't put the blame on the luxury brands. It is the job of a brand custodian to keep increasing these quotients. The onus is on the consumer – whether to take it on the dark side or not. But, that is true even for science.

Luxury brands should appeal to both the dark and bright sides.

Even the moon has a dark side.

Luxury: The Great Escape

"Great men are like eagles, and build their nest on some lofty solitude."

– Arthur Schopenhauer

Luxury, in its various forms, acts as a great escape. Luxury is a great partner for solitude. A few years back I had a conversation with our Union Finance Minister Mr Arun Jaitley on his penchant for luxury writing instruments for a story I was doing on lawyers and their liking for writing instruments. It is a well-guarded secret and very few people know about his brilliant collection. When we started the conversation he told me, "I just dictate and I am quite fast at that. I don't want to talk about it (the pen collection), it is a personal matter." However, after a little while when he realized that I want to know about his collection not as a journalist but as a fellow collector, he did open up a bit. And I did keep my word and kept it personal. Another senior politician and lawyer Abhishek Manu Singhvi is also not open to talk about his passion. "Yes, I do have a collection of writing instruments," he had told me during his interview for that story. The legal grapevine has it that he has also introduced some of his friends to fine writing instruments and has been successful in nursing a similar passion in them to full bloom.

What's with lawyers and luxury writing instruments? If you spot them at the courtrooms, you may find three sharpened HB pencils jutting out of their coat pockets. However, if you see them in their chambers, and sometimes at their homes, you will discover their secret passion. They are not very eager to talk about it or flaunt it, but if they discover that there is an appreciation for their collection, they open up and chat like a connoisseur would talk about his passion.

One escapes into luxury. Just like these lawyers and politicians, who only find time to dictate, secretly find solace in their collection of pens. They told me that in their busy schedules, they don't get any time for themselves. So they secretly take out an hour, may be an odd one, and spend time with their collection. They write, they clean and they fill the empty spaces with very interesting colours. "It is like meditation," a senior lawyer once told me.

The story is very similar with watch and clock collectors. I call them timekeepers. I have watched them closely ever since I was a child, secretly escaping into this luxury. My ancestral home has a great collection of antique luxury clocks and pocket watches. This was a collection that spanned three generations. Both my grandfather and his father, when they were alive, and now my father, spent one hour just winding all the clocks that included the grandfather's longcase, chimes, and pocket watches of the biggest brands, some dating back to the late 1800s. This was their private time, a time of solitude, no one was to enter the clock room for that one hour. They never boasted about their collection, it was very personal.

The case is very similar with connoisseurs of say cigar, single malt, and luxury/vintage cars. These are very personal and private escapades.

These escapades, if properly harnessed, are the next billion-dollar-churner for all luxury brands across the globe. They just need to recalibrate the positioning. Instead of positioning a brand meant for flaunting the logo where a customer will spend millions of dollars to show off, brand owners may position the brand as a great escape where consumers spend higher amounts to buy an escape from their busy and mundane lives where they do not have any personal time. They will eagerly pay top-dollar for that one hour a week, or that lazy private beach or yacht holiday, away from everyone, where the brand will be the lone companion to their luxury solitude.

Some guidelines for tapping this segment are as follows:

1. **Recalibrate your positioning:** Conceive branding opportunities wherein you sell solitude. However, the solitude should be very special. Always remember that it is luxury solitude, so the escape needs to be exquisite, say a private island.

2. **Align your communications with the target:** The advertisements or posters will not have "neighbour's envy owner's pride theme". It needs to have "spending quality time with oneself and with the brand". It needs to be very subtle and very personal. So all communication and creativity will fall in line with the idea of luxury escape or luxury solitude.

3. **Never exclude:** Men with means are the same people who also love to flaunt in some other aspects which

involve their family or their peers. And these are the same men who also seek expensive escapements for themselves. So never exclude one segment for another. So never say flaunters are bad or the other way round. Always remember: Every segment has its own class.

4. **Diversify your brand line:** The brand line needs to include products that cater to all kinds of buyers. Select and segregate very carefully which is best for solitude and which is best for flaunting.

5. **Mint the moolah:** As the solitude partner is an untapped and unorganized space where brand custodians have not given much attention to, this is the time to go for it and make the moolah.

Just escaping into luxury can make the brands richer by billions.

Luxury is the great escape.

Tailpiece
Timeless Tourbillons

"Ticking away the moments that make up
a dull day
Fritter and waste the hours in an off-hand way
Kicking around on a piece of ground in your
home town
Waiting for someone or something to show
you the way..."

– Pink Floyd (Time)

Time along with its movement has always been one of the greatest mysteries that have kept great minds occupied over ages. Equally mysterious and engaging are the ways to capture time. The human mind is attracted to complications and complicated movements, for it challenges the brain, just like a puzzle. Watchmakers have been designing complications in their desire to attain precision. However, the irony is that a mechanical watch, by definition, has to have imperfections. It has been a 400-year-old pursuit for the perfect time.

Each timeless timepiece is handcrafted painstakingly by timekeepers and watchmen who have kept the centuries' old tradition alive. Every wheel is balanced with precision, every gem is placed with perfection (to minimise friction). Without that precision, a watch can lose time.

My favourite example of the extent of a man's attachment to his watch is narrated in a story by the great filmmaker and author Satyajit Ray. The protagonist Thomas Godwin has had his favourite Perigal repeater buried with him.

Repeater is a movement. It was invented because in king's court it was not considered courteous to look at your pocket watch. In a repeater, if you press the crown, the watch gives out a soft sound that tells you the minute position. Swiss watchmakers have kept the repeater alive. Patek Phillipe, Jaeger-LeCoultre and Jaquet Droz still make repeaters.

Watch mechanisms and movements such as Retrograde are complex. Tourbillon, however, undoubtedly is the most complex of them all. It is an add-on in the mechanics of a watch escapement. Developed in 1795 by the French-Swiss watchmaker Abraham-Louis Breguet on an earlier idea of the English chronometer maker John Arnold, a Tourbillion counters the effects of gravity (yes, that also affects timekeeping) by mounting the escapement and balance wheel in a rotating cage. This nullifies the effects of gravity when the timepiece (and thus the escapement) is rotated.

Breguet made it because pocket watches were held in upright position in the pocket and not in the horizontal position, where the balances should ideally be, and thus the watches lost time due to gravity.

Breguet, Jaeger-LeCoultre, Harry Winston, and Cartier produce Master and Grandmaster Tourbillions. A modification in the movement of a Tourbillion takes up to five years to develop at Cartier. The Rotonde de Cartier single push-piece tourbillion sapphire skeleton is still the most sought-after piece from the company.

In 2004, Jaeger-LeCoultre created the Gyrotourbillon, more suitable for wristwatches, which see more movements than pocket watches. It is a two-axis, three-dimensional movement that compensates for the effect of gravity.

Mahatma Gandhi used a Zenith pocket watch. But he had no pockets as he was always in a loincloth. So the watch was slung from the waist tuck-in. He may not be aware, but his watch would have surely lost time, as gravity would tend to slow it down more than it would have in a pocket.

The jewel used in a Tourbillon is ruby. Jaeger-LeCoultre and Cartier use between seventeen and twenty-five rubies in each Tourbillon. Rubies give greater precision and accuracy. Their very small size and weight, low and predictable friction, good temperature withstanding ability, and the ability to operate without lubrication in corrosive environments make them key to watch-making. Mechanical watches also use diamond, sapphire, and garnet. It takes years of experience to know exactly where to place a jewel – the cap, pivot, impulse, or the centre wheel. No wonder a Tourbillon costs the moon – or somewhere near about. It can be anywhere between INR 50 lakh and INR 3 crore. But by no means it is the costliest watch money can buy. It's not easy to identify one, as buying one is almost always a closed-door affair. They don't carry price tags and prices are revealed only on request. And only to select customers. For viewing – much less buying one – an appointment for special preview needs to be sought. That's the standard practice with every luxury watchmaker. Neither the model, nor the price – forget about the identity of the customer – is revealed.

Should you want to take a look at the Opus collection or a Histoire de Tourbillon, you need to seek an appointment. Depending on who you are, it can be arranged at the Harry Winston boutique. That's only for a look-see; buying comes later. Harry Winston's Tourbillon range starts at over INR 80 lakh and goes up to INR 3 crore.

Jaeger-LeCoultre makes fifteen Gyrotourbillons a year, of which two are sold in India. People attracted to those kinds of pieces in India are usually corporate professionals who have travelled the world and are in their mid-forties to mid-fifties.

True, not many Indian Thomas Godwins are there who would want to take their watches to their graves. But, tourbillions or not, the legion of true blue Swiss watch aficionados in India is growing.

And thereby hangs a timeless tale.

Epilogue

"Luxury in the details."

– Hubert de Givenchy

Brand Manual for a Luxury Retailer

India and China are very different markets for luxury retailing and thus cannot be clustered as emerging markets for these brands. The two markets are intrinsically different.

Unlike China, we are the old markets for luxury, since the time of Maharajas. Things have changed, the texture of the market has changed, and more so, luxury has become democratized. Besides the New Maharajas, there has been a rise of the GIMC and they have been the primary drivers. Also there is this category of customers who are luxury rich and asset poor – masses with means. In India, it is still a play on volume and value for money, and not so much on ticket size.

With the luxury market in China slowing down, luxury retailing in India is certainly the next big story. Luxury market in India is poised to grow at 25% from 2013 till 2018 and is likely to touch $18-billion mark from the ongoing level of $14 billion.

Dear retailer, following is a brand manual that encapsulates the essence of the book for you to establish or re-establish your luxury brand in the Indian market.

1. Fighting the challenges in luxury retailing:

a. **Realty:** The only big challenge so far to rapid expansion of luxury retail in India is the availability of the right real estate spaces to house international luxury brands. Apart from the few malls in the major metros such as DLF Emporio in New Delhi, The Palladium in Mumbai, The UB City in Bangalore, and the Quest in Kolkata, there have not been any other major developments.

There is a need for many more such retail options in other cities too as there is a far wider target audience residing in smaller towns and cities which has the propensity to buy luxury goods. The reason China is fifteen years ahead of us in terms of expansion of luxury stores is purely because they have developed their infrastructure that supports this expansion.

b. **Space:** Luxury retailing cannot be confined to five star hotels as it is now widening the base to tap into a bigger pool in this country, the GIMC being the primary growth driver.

c. **Service versus product orientation:** Besides real estate, there is another issue and it is a deeper one: the perception of luxury. What people expect from luxury in India is very different from abroad. In the West, a bespoke suit is luxury, however, it isn't here and customers ask, "So, what else are you offering?" In India, luxury retailing is very service-oriented, while in the West it is product-oriented.

However, customers are also ready to forgo service if they are offered a discount instead. India is still a price-sensitive market.

d. **Adaptation is the mantra:** Every luxury retailer worth their salt is up for local adaptation to cut out a larger slice of the luxury pie. It gives so much comfort to walk into a Llardo boutique and see Rama, Sita, Ganesha, or Lakshmi created so beautifully with porcelain or to see the Hermes saree.

2. *Understanding luxury consumers*

a. **The experientialists:** This genre typically values new and exciting experiences more than buying products or brands. They spend on the experiences.

b. **The connoisseurs:** This genre is passionate in certain areas of interest and makes it a point to be well informed and knowledgeable about it. These categories could be art, scotch, wine, watches, writing instruments, cigars, horses, and the likes.

c. **The flaunters:** They are the force that drives luxury in India. They tend to value brand name over all other factors. Purchase of a brand is a sign of their status in the society and so visibility of the brand name is important. Badge seekers are seen mostly with the newly rich or new money class, especially among their young members.

d. **The aesthetes:** To this genre, the brand is much less important than the design. Aesthetes are luxury consumers purely because they have arrived at a stage of income at which they can indulge in their love for design among luxury brands or products. They will shell out a bomb because the object of desire is hand-stitched and not because of the label. They pride themselves for having an eye that picks out the unique and bold in design.

Built-in rationality and conservatism still dominates our minds, so one toe may be dipped in luxury, the other may be in a pool of value for money.

3. Everything is relative

a. In luxury branding "one size fits all" doesn't work. It is a space for bespoke, for customization, for making every customer feel special and justify the brand premium in pricing.

b. The biggest challenge that a luxury brand faces is in mixing the right portion of snob-value – not so much that you alienate others, but can't be so less that the clients don't feel the exclusivity. The magic potion lies in the right portion. It is both the presence and the absence of snob-quotient, both co-existing, side by side.

c. You need to have low-hanging accessories like sun glasses or perfumes or key chains or coin purses or scarves or what have you. They will lure a genre of clients who are heavy spenders in premium brand space and are yet to turn big spenders in luxury space, as they are not yet sure of the return on their investment, neither are they sure of the value for money for the product. So for them, these low-hanging fruits are only value for label.

d. With time, this customer segment realises the efficacy of the entire experience of luxury shopping, it is just not the product, it is the experience that you pay a premium for. Experiential luxury needs to be the unique selling proposition. Again to some it is worth the buck, to others it may not be. Therefore a retailer needs to provide the entire eco-system that provides a holistic luxury shopping experience.

4. *Brand ego*

a. It is all about being special or exclusive, to be someone who is not ordinary. Of being able to dazzle or luxe. Of being able to stand out in the crowd. This razzle-dazzle industry thrives on ego.

b. The idea that a marketeer sells is the exclusivity of the luxury brand and the exclusiveness of its owner. You will belong to an elite club such as a Lamborghini Club, flaunting your way in society.

c. The sheer arrogance that a brand exudes using prohibitive pricing to crowd out clients will make it aspirational. So the users will get an elevated feeling that he or she is part of an exclusive club. A brand such as Rolex is selling a legacy, a life of greatness, a masculine ego that craves for being distinguished.

5.   The Great Indian Middle Class: The strongest driver

Major luxury brands owe their existence to the GIMC. The secret behind the survival of high-brow luxury brands is the play in volumes. Shopping malls, in order to lure the middle class towards luxury and to give them its taste, are mixing luxury, super premium, and premium in the same shopping mall. You can't afford to restrict luxury retailing for five stars and exclude this group as they are your lifeline.

It is this aspiration that has led to the exponential rise of the market of knock-offs and first copies.

To sell or not to sell to the masses? That has been the big question that all retailers of luxury brands face.

Most of them have been struggling to strike a balance. The key lies in pricing. But the entire process has a few elaborate steps:

a.   Identify your signature products and add a premium for that signature. They are not for the GIMC to buy, but they constitute their aspirations. These products will always be displayed on the boutiques, mostly their pictures. Signature products are always out of stock and a fresh stock is always on its way from an antique land. This makes the GIMC keep coming back.

b. Identify the products that you want the New Maharajas to buy. Special edition pieces that are handcrafted should be there for display so that they can feel it and then take it home. These have a premium attached to them due to their exclusivity.

c. And then there are products that are masstige. They are to whet the appetite of the GIMC, so they can flaunt the logos of brands they always aspired to buy.

The most interesting part is that these companies never advertise to this category, so there is no brand dilution. The GIMC, however, advertises and brands these products to the other target audience in the same category, all for free. So the companies generate strong brand pull with this segment. And importantly, the aspiration lives on and grows.

6. *Democratization of luxury: The rise and rise of masstige*

a. Today, even the luxury of royalty is available for a price. How does it matter if you are not born in a Jaipur palace? Today, royal weddings have become commonplace. Perhaps the opening of palaces for hotels is the biggest step towards democratization of exclusivity of royalty. You will be treated like a king, if you have the moolah. Royal life is just a swipe away.

b. Now let us look at the rise of the so-called masses. This new category of customers are masses with means, luxury-rich but asset-poor. They are both an opportunity and a threat to the traditional luxury goods producers. As consumers, they are more demanding, more selective, and show less brand loyalty than the high net worth individuals who were the archetypal consumers of the old luxury. They are willing to pay high prices, but they expect commensurate quality; old luxury was never so fussy.

And they want the hottest, trendiest designs, which increasingly have to be marketed in creative (and expensive) ways.

These luxury-rich but asset-poor clients are the hottest for all luxury retailers and need to be wooed with royalty and exclusivity.

The masses – with and without means – along with the New Maharajas are your target, dear luxury retailer, in this high growth market.

Let your quest for luxury continue.

for a leading newspaper. His columns, interviews and quotes regularly appear in leading national media. He is a regular speaker on luxury brands, communications, branding, entrepreneurship and cinema and takes sessions at leading institutes such as IIM-Calcutta and IIT-KGP, industry bodies and forums such as CII and ASSOCHAM.

Hailing from a Brahmo family in Kolkata, Mahul is a student of St Xavier's College, Calcutta and is currently pursuing executive management programme from MICA. He is a rank-holder in Masters in International Economics from University of Calcutta. He is also pursuing his Ph.D. in Economics.

You can write to him at mahul@mahulbrahma. com.

About the author

Mahul has been a Senior Editor with leading media houses such as India partner of *New York Times-Financial Chronicle, The Economic Times,* Reuters and CNBC TV18. He is a columnist and commentator on luxury brands with *The Economic Times – ET Retail.* His earlier assignments include editing Op-Ed and Edit pages.

Mahul's debut short film as an actor has been selected and screened at the 69th Cannes Film Festival in 2016 and has won the Best Short Film title at the film festival in Boston. His feature film is due for release later this year.

He won "Ecommerce Communication Leader of the Year" Award in 2017. He is also the winner of "Young Achiever Award" in the coveted National Awards for Excellence in Communication in 2016.

He heads branding and corporate communications for a Tata Steel and SAIL venture – mjunction. He was formerly with Ambuja Neotia Group and RP-SG Group, heading corporate communications and branding.

An expert in luxury, besides commentating on luxury, Mahul has edited a luxury supplement